Butterfly Counting

Jerry Pallotta

Shennen Bersani

Charlesbridge

To Linda's pals: Katie Megan, Honor O'Hara, Archana Jairam, Elisabeth Costigan, Katie Elliott, and Senna Colace—J. P.

To my Corner Studio friends: Donna Berger, June Goulding, and Barbara Lanza—S. B.

Published by Charlesbridge
85 Main Street
Watertown, MA 02472
(617) 926-0329
www.charlesbridge.com

Library of Congress Cataloging-in-Publication Data
Pallotta, Jerry, author.
   The butterfly counting book/Jerry Pallotta; illustrated by Shennen Bersani.
      pages cm
   ISBN 978-1-57091-414-0 (reinforced for library use)
   ISBN 978-1-57091-415-7 (softcover)
   ISBN 978-1-60734-719-4 (ebook)
   ISBN 978-1-60734-638-8 (ebook pdf)
1. Counting—Juvenile literature. 2. Butterflies—Juvenile literature.
I. Bersani, Shennen, illustrator. II. Title.
QA113.P3414 2015
513.2'11—dc23   2013049018

Printed in China
(hc) 10 9 8 7 6 5 4 3 2
(sc) 10 9 8 7 6 5 4 3 2 1

Illustrations done in Prismacolor pencils on Arches watercolor paper
   and manipulated in Photoshop
Display type set in Liam designed by Laura Worthington
Text type set in Periodico
Color separations by KHL Chroma Graphics, Singapore
Printed by Jade Productions in Heyuan, Guangdong, China
Production supervision by Brian G. Walker
Designed by Susan Mallory Sherman

0
zero

This Emperor penguin has never seen a butterfly. Butterflies live in North America, South America, Europe, Asia, Australia, and Africa—but there are zero butterflies in Antarctica. Zero is a number, but it has no value.

Let's learn what butterflies are called around the world. A butterfly in Italy is called a *farfalla*.

10
ten

Count the butterflies. One, two, three, four, five, six, seven, eight, nine, ten. We counted to ten.

Now let's count to twenty. Eleven, twelve, thirteen, fourteen, fifteen, sixteen, seventeen, eighteen, nineteen, twenty. But wait . . . these are not butterflies! These are all moths. We tricked you! Moths can be very colorful. In Spanish, a butterfly is called a *mariposa*.

20
twenty

1
one

Let's start counting again with one. Here is one red Zarinda. Butterflies do not have a mouth with teeth. They have a curly proboscis. They use it like a straw to sip liquid.

In Japan, a butterfly is called a *choucho*.

2
two

Count the two Holly Blue butterflies. One, two.
Butterflies have two antennae. They use them
to smell.

The Polish word for butterfly is *motyl*.

3
three

Here are three green Cloudless Sulphur butterflies. Butterflies have three main body parts—a head, a thorax, and an abdomen.

By the way, a butterfly is called a *farasha* in Arabic.

4
four

These four purple butterflies are called Amethyst Hairstreaks. Butterflies have four wings—two forewings and two hind wings.

The Hawaiian word for butterfly is *pulelehua*.

5
five

Let's count the five Julias. There are about twenty thousand different species of butterflies, with hundreds of different wing shapes. Which shape do you like best?

The word for butterfly in Russian is *babochka*.

6
six

Here are six black Great Mormons. Butterflies are insects. All insects have six legs, which are attached to their thorax. Butterflies taste with their feet.

In the Hebrew language, a *parpar* is a butterfly.

7
seven

These seven butterflies are called Florida Whites. Butterflies do not fly in a straight line. The slightest breeze affects them. They fly erratically, crookedly, and twistingly—they are zigzaggy, jumpy, bumpy, and fluttery! This helps them avoid predators.

The Swahili word for butterfly is *vipepeo*.

8
eight

These eight Pink-tipped Clearwings have see-through forewings and pink hind wings. Being transparent is a great way for these butterflies to camouflage themselves.

In the Tagalog language, the word for butterfly is *paruparo*.

9
nine

These nine yellow butterflies are called Tailed
Sulphurs. Many species of butterflies are yellow.
Butter is also yellow. Is this where the word
"butterfly" came from?

The Mandarin Chinese word for butterfly is *hudie*.

10

ten

Count the ten Orions. One, two, three, four, five, six, seven, eight, nine, ten! Red, blue, green, purple, orange, black, white, pink, yellow, brown. Did you notice? We just learned ten numbers, ten colors, and a bunch of butterfly nature facts.

A butterfly in Germany is called a *schmetterling*.

11
eleven

Let's count higher and look at some multicolored butterflies. These eleven butterflies are called White Admirals. When butterflies land, they pull their wings up. A butterfly is called a *vlinder* in Dutch.

Enjoy these twelve Blue Triangles. It is common for Blue Triangles and other butterflies to drink from mud puddles. Lepidopterists call this mud-puddling. A lepidopterist is a scientist who studies butterflies and moths.

The Finnish word for butterfly is *perhonen*.

12
twelve

13
thirteen

These are thirteen Mourning Cloaks. Snakes, fish, moths, and lizards have scales. Butterflies have scales, too— on their wings. Most people don't think of butterflies as scaly creatures.

People in Portugal call a butterfly a *borboleta*.

14
fourteen

Count the fourteen Yellow Pansies. It is not a good idea to touch butterfly wings. They are fragile. It is not powder or dust that comes off the wings. It is a butterfly's scales.

In Greece, a butterfly is called a *petalouda*.

15
fifteen

Here are fifteen Queen of Spain Fritillaries.
Butterflies breathe through openings in their
abdomens called spiracles.
Butterflies are called *fidrildi* in Iceland.

16
sixteen

Count the sixteen Ghost Brimstones.
Don't be afraid. A butterfly cannot bite or
pinch you. It cannot scratch or sting.
Butterflies have no teeth, no fangs,
no sharp toenails, and no stingers.
   A butterfly in France is called a *papillon*.

17

seventeen

There are seventeen Blue Eyemarks here.
The word for butterfly poop is "frass."
In Denmark, a butterfly is called a *sommerfugl*.

Say hello to eighteen Giant Swallowtails. The color and design on the top side of butterfly wings is almost always completely different than the underside.

The sign for "butterfly" in many sign languages is made by interlocking your thumbs and flapping your hands like wings.

18
eighteen

19
nineteen

Count the nineteen Striped Blue Crows. Guess
what? There is no such thing as a baby butterfly.
All butterflies are adults. Let's learn about the life
cycle of a butterfly next.
A butterfly in Korea is called a *nahbee*.

20
twenty

Count the twenty Pipevine Swallowtail butterfly eggs. The life cycle of a butterfly is one of nature's marvels. It starts when a butterfly lays eggs on a leaf. The leaf will be food for the eggs when they hatch.

The Malaysian word for butterfly is *rama-rama*.

21
twenty-one

Butterfly eggs hatch into caterpillars. Caterpillars come in all different shapes, sizes, and colors. The illustrator painted twenty-one different species here. These caterpillars will eat and eat and eat and get big and fat.

K'aalógii means butterfly in the Navajo language.

Here are twenty-two chrysalises. A caterpillar pupates into a chrysalis and later transforms into an adult butterfly. Look, two Blue Morphos have just emerged. The top side of their wings is blue, and the underside is brown.

In Romanian, a butterfly is known as a *fluture*.

23
twenty-three

The life cycle of a butterfly is called metamorphosis. The word "metamorphosis" means "transformation." These twenty-three Dido Longwings have transformed from egg to caterpillar to chrysalis to butterfly.

In Taiwanese, a butterfly is called an *o'tiap*.

Just for a day, would you like to be one of these twenty-four Peacock butterflies? Here is the deal: to become a beautiful butterfly, you have to be an ugly caterpillar first.

The Turkish name for butterfly is *kelebek*.

If you were the first person to find this butterfly, what would you call it? Piano Keys is the perfect name, isn't it? In New Zealand, the native Maori call a butterfly a *pepeké*.

Zero, one, two, three, four, five, six, seven, eight, nine, ten, eleven, twelve, thirteen, fourteen, fifteen, sixteen, seventeen, eighteen, nineteen, twenty, twenty-one, twenty-two, twenty-three, twenty-four, twenty-five butterflies . . . and one penguin!

A butterfly in Great Britain is called a butterfly. But don't be silly! This is not a butterfly. It is a grasshopper. Should we write a grasshopper book next?